COOKIES

by Emily Jenkins

SAMUEL FRENCH

samuelfrench.co.uk

FOR AMATEUR PRODUCTION ENQUIRIES

UNITED KINGDOM AND WORLD
EXCLUDING NORTH AMERICA
plays@samuelfrench.co.uk
020 7255 4302/01

Each title is subject to availability from Samuel French,
depending upon country of performance.

Acting Editions

BORN TO PERFORM

Playscripts designed from the ground up to work the way you do in rehearsal, performance and study

---

Larger, clearer text for easier reading

Wider margins for notes

Performance features such as character and props lists, sound and lighting cues, and more

---

+ CHOOSE A SIZE AND STYLE TO SUIT YOU

STANDARD EDITION

Our regular paperback book at our regular size

SPIRAL-BOUND EDITION

The same size as the Standard Edition, but with a sturdy, easy-to-fold, easy-to-hold spiral-bound spine

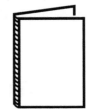

LARGE EDITION

A4 size and spiral bound, with larger text and a blank page for notes opposite every page of text – perfect for technical and directing use

---

LEARN MORE   **samuelfrench.co.uk/actingeditions**

MUSIC USE NOTE

Licensees are solely responsible for obtaining formal written permission from copyright owners to use copyrighted music in the performance of this play and are strongly cautioned to do so. If no such permission is obtained by the licensee, then the licensee must use only original music that the licensee owns and controls. Licensees are solely responsible and liable for all music clearances and shall indemnify the copyright owners of the play(s) and their licensing agent, Samuel French, against any costs, expenses, losses and liabilities arising from the use of music by licensees. Please contact the appropriate music licensing authority in your territory for the rights to any incidental music.

USE OF COPYRIGHT MUSIC

A licence issued by Samuel French Ltd to perform this play does not include permission to use the incidental music specified in this copy.

Where the place of performance is already licensed by the PERFORMING RIGHT SOCIETY (PRS) a return of the music used must be made to them. If the place of performance is not so licensed then application should be made to the PRS, 2 Pancras Square, London, N1C 4AG.

A separate and additional licence from PHONOGRAPHIC PERFORMANCE LTD, 1 Upper James Street, London W1F 9DE (www.ppluk.com) is needed whenever commercial recordings are used.

IMPORTANT BILLING AND CREDIT REQUIREMENTS

If you have obtained performance rights to this title, please refer to your licensing agreement for important billing and credit requirements.

ABOUT THE AUTHOR

Emily is a winner of the prestigious Fringe First Award for her play *Rainbow*. She has since written plays for Paines Plough, Traverse Theatre and attended the Royal Court Young Writers and Studio Writers programmes.

Emily is also a text coach and Shakespeare practitioner working at Shakespeare's Globe Theatre. Her productions for Shakespeare's Globe include *The Tempest* (Dir. Jeremy Herrin), *A Midsummer Night's Dream* (Dir. Dominic Dromgoole) and *King Lear* (Dir. Bill Buckhurst). She also teaches at LAMDA and has worked as text coach for the National Youth Theatre company. Productions as text and voice coach include *Romeo and Juliet* for the Ambassadors Theatre (Dir. Katy Hewitt) and *The Tempest* for Royal & Derngate (Dir. Caroline Steinbeis).

As a director her work includes: *Vinegar Tom* (Royal and Derngate Theatre), *Merry Wives of Windsor* (Royal and Derngate studio), *KCS* (Southwark Playhouse), *Rainbow* (FRINGE FIRST AWARD WINNER Zoo Southside), *Mojo Mickybo* (Old Red Lion) and *Fame* (The Northcott Theatre).

AUTHOR'S NOTE

When I was approached to write this play I wasn't sure I was the best person to do it. Apart from WhatsApp I barely used any social media at all; I'd left Facebook 6 years previously when I got sick of looking at how much fun everyone seemed to be having – ALL the time – without me. I wasn't much better on Twitter: terrified of trolls or any negative comments I was – and am still – the queen of the retweet; happily preaching to the converted within my liberal bubble.

All in all, I was desperately out of the social media loop.

Saying that, I still think of myself as part of the first social media generation. Facebook came to the UK around my first year at university. At the time it was just a private network of university students, serving as a way to share photos and arrange nights outs before iPhones and smart phones properly got going. However, within a few years that small network of students had grown bigger and bigger, and before we knew it there were no walls between ourselves, our photos, and the rest of the world. It was a sneak attack that took us years to understand.

So the thought of writing a play about a world I had intentionally excluded myself from felt rather presumptuous.

That was where 150 incredible students between the ages of 16 and 19 came in. As part of the Cyberscene project, students from colleges around London were invited to take part in a series of drama workshops about cyber-safety. I had the privilege of sitting in on these workshops and interviewing many of these young people. I quickly realised (perhaps I should have sooner) that this play wasn't about my experiences, it was about theirs. And it is from them that this play comes.

This play is an amalgamation of many stories that were shared with me. Some shocking, some moving, some terrifying, some told to me as if it was completely normal whilst I gawped at the things these young people were already exposed and desensitised to.

And that's the thing – as much as technology has made our lives easier, I think it has made growing up much, much harder; now there are two worlds to navigate simultaneously. And it is because of that, for many, there is no escape from the pressures of school, friends, identity, sex, parents, and everything else you're trying to juggle whilst figuring out who the hell you are and trying to get the best grades possible for that elusive 'future' adults keep going on about. What's worse is, if you are bullied or having a hard time at school, home is no longer an escape. The harsh words don't disappear at the end of the school day. They're there 24/7 on your phone and computer screen. There is no automatic safe space for young people anymore and that is something we need to acknowledge.

The internet is also less forgiving: a single mistake isn't eventually forgotten, it exists online forever. Pain and memories fade, but pixels don't; wounds are never allowed to heal. As one student said to me "It's like a warzone. I feel like I might constantly be attacked, I don't know how to escape."

Speaking of attacks, it was not only the students that contributed to the narratives within this play, but the atmosphere in which I was writing. I was commissioned at the end of 2016. Over the course of the following year we were subject to a series of horrific terrorist attacks on this country and across Europe, in the UK starting with the Westminster attack and shortly followed by Manchester and London Bridge and a mosque in Finsbury Park, among others. Although the attack that is mentioned in the Rayah / Salena storyline is fictional, these real life events are deeply connected to the journey of the play. The attacks themselves were shocking, but what was even more terrifying to me was the prejudice, persecution and racism that it engendered towards many ethnic and religious groups, particularly Muslims, in the weeks and months (and now years) after. Many of the young people I talked to had experienced this first hand – both online and off – due to their religion, the colour of their skin, their sexual orientation, a disability or a million other ridiculous reasons. It became vitally important to me to show that the continuing and constant persecution of anyone considered different from yourself only creates further social isolation and division. This is why the play begins with the moment on the bus, and this is why Rayah becomes the only person Salena feels that she can talk to. It is a feeling of isolation and rejection in the real world that causes someone to turn to a stranger on the internet, and it is a simple act of kindness by a stranger in real life that leads to Salena's salvation. If we could all make a small gesture of kindness towards someone we don't know, every day, perhaps things might be different? I hope so.

The other thing to say about the Salena / Rayah storyline in particular is that, although it discusses extremism, it is at its core a story of online grooming. The way Rayah befriends Salena and becomes her confidante then manipulates her into making a life-altering decision, is something that many young people have experienced. Whether the result is sharing naked photos online, revealing personal information about themselves, having their beliefs manipulated, or meeting their online 'friend' for the first time with disastrous consequences, the process of grooming is always the same regardless of the perpetrator's end goal.

And that brings me to the final thing I want to share. Throughout this process I was inspired by the honesty and bravery of the young people that I spoke to. There are many conversations, people and moments that I will never forget, but there is one moment that became the driving force behind writing this play. It was during a conversation with one young woman, very early on in the process. We had been talking for over two hours about her experiences and I was coming to the end of my questions. The final question, as I asked all those I spoke to, was:

"What do YOU think this play should be about?"

She looked at me for a moment with surprise before replying:

"I don't mind, exactly. We just want to be listened to. No one ever listens to us."

I hope that she, and other young people who read, or see, or perform this play, will connect to the characters and in their own way, feel heard. They are the experts in their own experiences and perhaps as adults we spend a little too much time talking at young people, rather than listening. They are smarter and more astute than they are ever given credit for. I've tried my hardest with this play to listen without judgement. And make sure it is their voices that speak, not mine. Every character in this play makes a mistake that changes theirs, or another's life, irrevocably. But a mistake doesn't make you a bad person – look at Simon or Eva or anyone in the play, really – it makes you human. And rather than telling them what not to do, we can encourage future generations to forgive themselves and move forward and perhaps not make that mistake again. If this play can contribute even a little to a conversation where we properly listen to young people's voices, then every single minute of this process will have been worth it.

Emily Jenkins
November 2018

COOKIES received its world premiere at the Theatre Royal Haymarket on Sunday, 29 October 2017. It was produced by the Theatre Royal Haymarket Masterclass Trust in partnership with The Pureland Foundation and Kidscape with the following cast and creatives:

SIMON	Makir Ahmed
EVA	Cristal Cole
ANDY	Bradley Cumberbatch
SOSA	Leaphia Darko
SALENA	Rujenne Green
RAYAH	Shala Nyx
JC	Joe Pierson

STUDENT ENSEMBLE

Barnet & Southgate College
Naseem Hosany

Leyton Sixth Form College
Johnson Adebayo | Nesmie K Constantine
Shiri Fileman | Dorant Gjocaj
Christopher Jason Quagraine | Bianca Rawlinson
George Sicobo | Natalia Szymaniak

Hackney Community College
Michael Alake | Lekan Ayemojuba
Jessica Lima | Doridan Nahoum Bavangila
Brandon Thorne | Damien Zdrale

South Thames College
Isatou Dibaga | Harry Phillips
Tomasz Stefanski

Playwright	Emily Jenkins
Director	Anna Ledwich
Set and Costume Designer	Frankie Bradshaw
Sound Designer and Composer	Max Pappenheim

Lighting Designer	Elliot Griggs
Projection Designer	Nina Dunn
Movement Director	Natasha Khamjani
Casting Director	Ellie Collyer-Bristow
Production Manager	Luke Child
Company Stage Manager	Jasmin Hay
Deputy Stage Manager	Lynsey Fraser
Assistant Stage Manager	Zhe Cui
Design Assistant	Emily Adamson
Artistic Adviser	Jonathan Church CBE
Creative Producer	Rhiannon Newman Brown
Production Coordinator	Lucy Curtis
Project Evaluation	Dr Ellen Helsper, LSE
Cyberscene Development Director	Guy Unsworth
Cyberscene Workshop Leaders	Hazel Gould
	Arne Polhmeier
	Joy Richardson
Education Resources	Lucy Curtis
	Susie Ferguson
Marketing and Press	Josh Brown
	Danielle Morgan-Dodd
	Georgie Anderson, Ellen Walpole
	Jazz Adamson
Videography	William Geraghty
Press	Chloe Nelkin Consulting
Production Photography	Pamela Raith
Cyberscene Ambassadors	Lady Viola Grosvenor
	Maddy Hill, Ted Reilly

Thanks to all the students and teachers* from the four colleges who participated in the original Cyberscene workshops from October 2016

Barnet & Southgate College
Samuel Appiah-Twum
Oliver Balshaw
Ashlee Chisakuwana
Roxana Dumitrache
Sharmin Fattahi
Aaliyah Frustaci
Daniela Gomes
Ibrahin Hiis
Karishma Khatry
Hamza Modhafar
Isaac Charles Morrison
Victoria Pohlmann
Andreia Santos
Love Siega
Sean Welsh
*Linda Julian
*Laura Sampson

Leyton Sixth Form College
Sara Banas
Tyrell Browne
Charlotte Danso
Ethan Dawkins
Laeticia Gassa
Ezekiel Hardie
Tawny Harding
Juanisha Howard
Elena Ionita
Joseph Jackman
Lucie Lutte
Timiera Lynck
Bianca Manea
Timothy Mascoll
Lauryn Nicole Reid
*Katy Arnell
*Justin Pierre

Hackney Community College
Al Amin
Alana Barnard
Kejenne Beard
Zsofi Borbely
Hannah Browning
Finnian Burnett Pope
Aran Celikdemir
Mia Christian-Law
Valentina Coley
Cheyenne Damioli
Esther Edgal
Ahai Foster
Kailyn George
Tamara Green
Deshan Griffith
Brogan Neal
Rachael Okai
Shannon Phelan
Graciela Pinto
Kelan Ryan
Rebeca Texeira
Holly Watson Abell
Shantelle Williams
*Pippa Luce
*Frances Sexton

South Thames College
Rachael Adechi
Shola Ajala
Razia Akram
Ahmad Al-Saadon
Euriza Amin Salman
Kafayat Awosile
Emily Barton
Dinara Chasanova
Ghita El Alaoui Sossi
Abir El Alaoui Sossi
Asore Ewers
Kevelin Fernandes
Hazia Gondal
Ana Lucia Mateus Ruiz
Hasnain Rehman
Rafiat Salami
Rahima Shafiq
Hayley Smith
Charlie Stokes
Kelly Ulloa
Ali Waheed
*Andrew Beardall
*Michael Helene

Programme Director	**Blayne George**
Programmer	**Hazel Kerr**
Press and Marketing Manager	**Josh Brown**
Marketing and Design Assistant	**Ellen Walpole**
Programming and Development Assistant	**Jazz Adamson**

Chief Executive	**Lauren Seager-Smith**
Director of Services	**Peter Bradley**
Training and Development Manager	**Yvonne Richards**
Website, Print and Database Manager	**Richard Andrew**
Fundraising Officer	**Jill Taylor**
Extremism and Radicalisation Awareness Project Manager	**Jade Gayle**
Communications Manager	**Zoe Williams**

PURELAND FOUNDATION

Founder	**Bruno Wang**

CYBERSCENE AND COOKIES

COOKIES was commissioned as part of Cyberscene, a theatre initiative created by Blayne George, Programme Director of the Theatre Royal Haymarket Masterclass Trust as a way of using theatre to help explore, understand and raise awareness of the intricate complexities of growing up in a digital world. *COOKIES* was written with young people for young people with the aim of giving a group of 16 – 19 year olds a unique platform to share their thoughts and experiences of cyber bullying and the effects the wider online world is having on their lives. Cyberscene was the recipient of the Security Serious Unsung Heroes Award's 'Best Security Awareness Campaign' award for 2018.

Cyberscene, *COOKIES* and *COOKIES:* The Film were made possible through the generous support of The Pureland Foundation and the Theatre Royal Haymarket

COOKIES: THE FILM – masterclass.org.uk/view/cookies-the-film

Watching the film of *COOKIES* combined with the free comprehensive education resource packs, which have been developed in line with the AQA's GCSE and A-Level Drama and PSHE Association Curriculum, will help teachers enrich their students' learning and educational experience.

The education pack can be found at masterclass.org.uk/view/cookies-educational-resources-

The characters in this play are fictional and reflect real experiences and opinions gathered from the Cyberscene student participants as well as events of 2016/17. The Masterclass and Kidscape teams have supported the playwright to ensure that the information around the legality of the actions depicted in the play are correct. Guidelines are interpreted differently across the U.K. and clarification on issues touched on in the play should be sought from your local police service or the experts listed below.

A FEW NOTES ON THE TEXT

STAGING

The seven main characters should remain onstage throughout. **RAYAH** should begin dressed similarly to **SALENA**. As the narrative progresses, her dress becomes more conservative.

CHORUS

The original production had a chorus of 20 young people. However, **CHORUS** lines can instead be divided between the main seven cast members. Unless otherwise instructed **CHORUS** lines should not be allocated via presumptions of gender.

The lines that are labelled as Verbatim can be cut if needed. They come from the interviews that inspired this play and are there to show how the three stories burst forth from all the hundreds of voices trying to share their experiences. In the original production they were recorded and used as a soundscape which worked really well. I would suggest keeping them, but they are not necessary to the plot. However, all other **CHORUS** lines must be kept in.

LANGUAGE

Online language is used in a slightly different way in each of the stories – sometimes to show distance, sometimes to show intimacy – but it should always be spoken as if the characters are in the same room.

Within the **EVA / SIMON** narrative when characters are communicating via text/WhatsApp/email, all punctuation marks (including full stops and commas) are spoken out loud – these are written into the dialogue.
For example: "What? What you waking me for?"
 is written as...
"What question What you waking me for question"

Rhyme, on the other hand, is the offline world where true thoughts and feelings can be expressed.

/ indicates a point of interruption.

TECHNOLOGY IS CHANGING

Most importantly, I'm sure most of the language or apps in this play are either already – or soon will be – out of date. Feel free to change these if you think different apps or phrases (or popstars) would work better!

CHARACTERS

SOSA – Female, Black, 17

SALENA – Female, Muslim, any ethnicity, 16
RAYAH – Female, Muslim, any ethnicity, 16

SIMON – Male, any ethnicity, 17
JC – Male, any ethnicity, 16
ANDY – Male, Muslim, any ethnicity, 17
EVA – Female, any ethnicity, 17
VOICE

CHORUS

All characters have grown up in the UK.
The cast should be as ethnically diverse as possible.

An empty stage. **VOICES** *fill the space. The following chorus speech is verbatim to be used at your discretion.*

CHORUS

Say,

 if I'm playing a game

 and I'm doing better than someone on the opposite team

  normally they message you saying

   "shut up. Go kill yourself. You're shit."

Sexting happens a lot

 a lot a lot a lot

  the kind of people who do it

   I would never do it myself

    / because it's exposed it's just out there for everyone to see

Social media added another level to bullying in secondary school

 cause it's harder to escape / you know?

My girlfriend never takes photos of herself without a filter

 I tell her she looks good in real life

  but she'll never take a photo without a filter

   coz it makes her feel better

    / like leaves the skin clearer

     like she can edit herself

You'll have people that are very old

 like thirty and stuff like that

messaging me

being like 'oh you're beautiful

can I meet you?

Dis dat dat'

I'm just there like

wait you don't have kids or wife like?

I'm young like /

I don't know you like

I've been bullied

I won't lie

I've bullied people before

like when I come to this country people said racist things /

stuff like that

We are in a warzone. It is not literal or realistic. It should be stylised and always feel urban and contemporary. Rap music and pop music join the voices and battlefield sounds.

CHORUS

Someone must have done dissed him

dya know what I mean by dissed him?

Like

mocked him in their music video on YouTube like

rapped about him and was like dis dat dat dat and den /

so he made another track to diss dem

and he had more views

dya know what I mean?

And if you're both musicians like dat

underground musicians

and you're dissing each other online

The not-so-cool people
  that's the people that's gonna get affected / the most
    but I guess it's just the fact that I'm more confident in myself
     so if I see someone wants to come bully me
      no
        I cut you off
          because I know what's meant to be
            and what's not meant to be
And it's not that simple with blocking them
  because they can always get to you through other people
   you know
     and they're at school with you and friends with you
       and they / know you're online

Now I feel that if you allow yourself to be bullied you will be bullied

But I said to her like
  like she looks good
    but having an app like this it makes people
      I don't know
        feel more comfortable
         like edit themselves
           make them feel better
               A lot of them not confident with who they are
               in real life

The sound builds and then suddenly stops leaving a single voice remaining... (Carrying on from "someone must have done dissed him...").

CHORUS
...dya know what I mean?
　And if you're both musicians like dat
　　underground musicians
　　　and you're dissing each other online

　End of verbatim speech.

　An explosion hits.

　　SOSA *is thrown towards the audience.*

SOSA　so i'm on the 333
　　and it's like jammed like
　　fucking
　　what's you call it
　　sardines
　　and i've got my buds in pumping pumping my girl MakDown
　　MD
　　straight into my brain my mind
　　drowning out the noise and the sound of babies crying
　　old men dying
　　young girls lying
　　to their mums and dads about where they're out to tonight
　　and the ping ping of the bus bell at every stop as the mums
　　do the pram shuffle and someone in a wheelchair tries to
　　get on

　　i block out the hell with the sound of my rapper in my ears
　　angry and like beautiful and dark

　　and right now it's like

i'm there

with my girl

MakDown

and we just know

you know

that all the pain
all the rage
all the dark damp of the streets
and the violence and the anger of our yout our generation
is just

music and rap and words and beats

i'm jumped out of my sound as i look around
and see this white guy's face
pressed out of place
against the gold dark skin of this girl in a headscarf

he gives this snorting laugh
and he whispers sumin in her ear
and with surprise

i see fear
in her eyes
before he licks his lips
and spits
right onto her cheek

"Go back to where you came from."

he says full loud
and then looking strong and proud
the little fuck bucks and ducks
out into the night
and the bus doors shut tight

the bus has frozen
shut down to a whisper
but not one person
looks to her
they all look away
carry on with their day

"Fuck this"
i say
and i plant my butt right down next to her
and i hold out my bud
"You like music blud?"

she hesitates and i wait
takes it in her hand and holds it straight
against her ear to hear

she gives me half a smile and together we sit
sharing the beat
as the lights blur in the street
we don't speak

but for the rest of the trip
our heads dip
in time to MakDown's rhymes
and with a fleeting glance i see a tear dance

down her cheek

my MakDown can speak

The voices build again within the warzone.

CHORUS *(verbatim)*

There's dangerous people on the internet

  like you don't know who you could start talking to like

  like you read all these things about

    about like grooming

      or whatsit called

There's a lot of stuff that's happened over my life because I've trusted the wrong people

  particularly online

   and like I believed what they told me

    and basically I got myself in some dangerous situations

I reached out

  because I didn't think anyone in my life understood me

   like like

    I got talking to this person

SALENA I'm riding high

   with my best friend by my side

   and we sing loud and proud as we please,

   our bags hitting our knees,

   and new look and accessorize prize

   fill our eyes,

   through Westfield corridors

and multiple floors.

We've been at the Nike Store
and I've just got my airs.
I've been wanting a pair
for like, ever.
I've been saving and now with my birthday money –
I'm sixteen wooo –
I finally got them!

I'm so excited I couldn't wait;
so I put them straight on,
and now we're roaming looking where next to hit
on our non-stop Saturday shop-til-we-drop.

New Nike airs squeak and smack black
as we sing at the top of our voices;
singing
and grinning,
and not caring who looks at us and what they say.

They sing part of the chorus of Zayn Malik's **"PILLOW
TALK".** *

I tweet a selfie of me and my girl
and the Zayn poster I just got.

I'm always on my phone
fan sites and twitter and such
Spreading Zayn love

Hashtag I heart Zayn so much.

RAYAH No hashtag I heart Zayn so much! He's so beautiful.

---

* A licence to produce *COOKIES does not include a performance licence for
"PILLOW TALK". For further information, please see Music Use Note on page v.*

SALENA Oh my God isn't he tho!

RAYAH Totally.

SALENA Like I genuinely want to marry him and have his babies.

RAYAH I know right. Have you seen that MTV pic of him he posted?

SALENA It's my screensaver.

RAYAH Mine too! Bruv, I am like THE biggest Zayn fan.

SALENA There's no way you love him more than me. I have like a million pictures on my phone. Bruv what's your favourite song?

The warzone becomes more realistic. Gunfire. Helicopters overhead.

Female voices.

CHORUS *(verbatim)*
It's like girls are like
  expected to look a certain way
    act a certain way
      so when you don't conform
        people are gonna put it on social / media and like

Sexting happens a lot
  a lot a lot a lot
    the kind of people who do it
      I would never do it myself
        / because it's exposed it's just out there for everyone to see.

For a girl it's literally like
  the end of your world

People ask me for pictures all the time

   Strangers

      boys at school

         I don't but like

Say my boyfriend breaks up with me

   and he thinks

      "oh I'm going to use that as revenge."

So then he is just an asshole

No one blames the guy for asking

   it's always the girl's fault

      if she's like stupid enough / to send it

The internet's like this

   this

      crazy warzone

         you know

   The warzone has become realistic. **JC** *and* **SIMON** *are*
   retreating soldiers amongst the gunfire and explosions.

JC We're moving out!

SIMON Let me take the shot!

JC Let's go let's go!

SIMON Let me take the shot!

JC There's no time. Let's go!

   An explosion hits.

   They are thrown backwards.

   Everything freezes.

SIMON *and* JC *emerge from the rubble.*

They have been playing the game in separate houses but their dialogue is quick fire and rapid; they speak as if they are in the same room.

SIMON Shit.

JC What the fuck. Any chance we could play one time without you getting hit.

SIMON We should have gone with the airstrike.

JC Yeh and somehow you'd still get hit.

SIMON Ah I missed this.

JC Yes mate. Glad you're back!

SIMON Yeh sorry I've been MIA.

JC She was a bitch. I never liked her.

SIMON Oh yeh? That why you asked her out last year?

JC Fuck you.

SIMON Just water in your eyes when she rejected you and went for me?

JC I dodged a bullet mate. Which is something you don't seem able to manage.

SIMON Yeh whatever.

JC I didn't want to say anything but I have heard sumin.

SIMON What?

JC Sure you wanna know?

SIMON JC. What?

JC Sure?

SIMON JC.

JC So don't shoot the messenger but apparently it's been going on since Shanna's party.

SIMON What had?

JC Duh. Her and Rob. That's where they first hooked up.

SIMON Bullshit.

JC What I heard.

SIMON Who said.

JC Salena told Shanna told Andy told me.

SIMON Bullshit.

JC Yeh but you left early didn't you.

SIMON Yeh. So.

JC So after you left...

SIMON But why?

JC Salena said you guys had a fight or sumin?

SIMON Yeh but –

JC So you left, she was pissed off...

SIMON Can't have.

JC Whilst they were singing happy birthday.

SIMON Bullshit.

JC What I heard.

SIMON Mate she sent me these that night –

   SIMON *sends some pictures to* JC.

JC No way mate!

SIMON Not the only ones she sent. My memory's like zero I've got so many.

   ANDY *appears.*

ANDY Request to join?

SIMON Andy's requesting to join.

SIMON Accept.

SOSA i not got much data left so
    i quick check the snapchat my girl's sent me
    flower crown filter
    new do

    she spent all day getting it done

    for this night
    tonight

    and she is looking peng

    we've not been friends long
    we just started chatting one day about shit
    and before we were aware of it
    we had delved into ourselves

    i even told her i'm into girls
    and she was totally cool

    i can't snap here so i whatsapp
    eye heart emoji
    one tick
    two tick
    two ticks blue

    then quick check MakDown's channel for comments on
    the new tune

it's gone down well
but as expected the rappers in south don't approve

threats of shanking
and take downs
and knives and guns
all down the comments section

and pieces of shit emojis
and water pistol
head
explosion

Makdown is north london
my london
the heart

their rapper down south just ain't
get me
just ain't

but this feud's been going forever

immature boys and their immature toys
even the wifeys and hood rats and skets
all try to get
in on the action
trying to shut her down
acting like clowns
saying she's no right to speak
she's too female and weak
or a whore or a dyke

but try all they might
she just rises above
smashing their hate with her truth and love
and it fucking scares them to death

war ain't just a man's game
i've seen sisters spill blood as quick as a bro

and having a girl a woman like MD
out there
for them all to see
up against these boys
these men
making music better than them
they can't stand it

and it ain't just on the streets no more
one video and the other slaps back
my music's better than yours my gangs gonna take yours
and sometimes they do

the internet is their battle ground
london their surround sound
youtube their statement maker their
whatsit
manifesto maker

but she's preaching sumin different
she's preaching something beautiful that
these clowns don't get

but i do

i know i do

because when i listen to her tunes

or watch her deep red beautiful lips

spit

it's like she's speaking direct to my soul

and for that brief sharp shock moment i feel whole

and for a second

my sister

my baby sister

my 13-year-old sister and her blood-soaked clothes by the railings of that park in the dark

disappears from the oxygen of my thoughts and i can breathe again

ANDY Alright gays! And Simon

SIMON Ha.

JC Andy it's not funny anymore. I'm not fucking gay.

SIMON You sure mate?

ANDY Not what I heard.

JC Fuck you.

ANDY Mate I'm flattered but you're not my type.

JC Yeh who is? Simon? You're so gay bet you're not even interested what Eva sent him. Look.

He sends the pictures.

ANDY What the – Man you know I'm not meant to be seeing this kind of shit at the moment.

SIMON You're not meant to be playing computer games either. Or swearing.

ANDY Yeh alright. Just don't tell my mum. When she send them?

JC Night she first cheated on our boy.

ANDY No way.

JC Yeh Salena told me.

ANDY She's gone a bit weird. I was at mosque last night and –

SIMON Boys, can we play?

ANDY *(about the picture)* Man Eva is fit tho.

> **EVA** *enters and begins dancing hip hop. In between the boys' lines she shouts instructions as she dances – what move is coming next etc. We realise she is demonstrating a dance routine on her YouTube channel. She is a very good amateur dancer.*

JC Dancer bod innit.

EVA Hip. Hip.

SIMON Yeh.

EVA Ripple it down.

ANDY Better off without her mate.

EVA Cross turn.

SIMON Can we play?

EVA Hip hip.

ANDY Hell yeh.

EVA Cross cross.

JC Let's blow some shit up!

EVA Wind it back.

ANDY Lock and load!

JC, ANDY, SIMON AND EVA Wooo!

The dance finishes.

EVA Great job everyone. Really great job! Woo! Way to swagger! Woo! That was intense.

So we've finally completed like the first ever Dance with Eva routine! Woo! Can't believe it!

Guys, I am like crazy proud of you for sticking with it. I feel like so blessed to have so many of you supporting me.

So next week next week we'll start learning a new one! With some like some like brand new hip hop moves that are sick.

And guys, if you haven't done it yet please make sure to follow me on Facebook at Dance with Eva and my handle, very easy like, @dancewithEva for new vid updates and extra dance instructions. And subscribe yeh subscribe!

So yeh. See you next time.
Eva Out.

Mwah

To audience.

I want to be a YouTube hit –

popular throughout the nation,

a dancing sensation.

With millions of hits and likes and high price merchandise

with my name all over it.

I could do appearances –

dance on stage with celebrities and pop stars,

appearances at clubs and bars,

and spend my whole life just doing dance.

But it's not just the glam –

dancing is me
it's who I am.
Dancing's the only time I don't want to scream and shout,
the only time I'm not filled with fear and doubt,
the only time I feel like I belong,

when my body's pumping to some banging song.

It's my way out.

I've just finished uploading another vid when my phone
starts to beep.

And then it beeps again.

And then it starts to ring.

It's one of my friends,

"Hey girl whats up?" I say.

She replies:

"Babe you been on Facebook? You need to look. Like now."

I open my phone.

What?

What?

My world stops.

Then suddenly my gut shuts and twists,
and plummets like a comet,
and then

my whole body vomits.

I press my hand hard against my lips,
trying to stop the overwhelming sick
spurting through fingers' chinks.
But before I get to the sink,
chunks of Walkers crisps and carrot sticks
explode out of me.

I wretch into porcelain and plumbing,
bent double,
my fingers pulling and thumbing my sick-sunk hair
as chunks of puke shoot out everywhere.

I'm there for an hour.

Until there's nothing left but yellow bile
and a pile of soaking towels by my side.

My body is tired and trembling,
I think my world is permanently ending.

RAYAH So how was your birthday? Did you have a good time
    yeh?

SALENA Oh my God bruv, so much fun. Like my friend Shanna
    had this amazing party for everyone at college, totally epic.
    And the next day we went to this waffle place which was
    like so banging.

RAYAH Where do you get that Zayn poster? I love that pic of him.

SALENA Yeh got that for my birthday. Shanna's dead jealous.
    I've put it on the wall right by my bed.

RAYAH Where's this waffle place?

SALENA You London yeh? Brixton bruv.

RAYAH No way! Like I literally grew up round the corner sister.

SALENA Serious!? Where you at!?

RAYAH Serious. I used to get the 333 there weekends.

SALENA Oh yeh? What stop you near?

RAYAH Just up the hill. My dad runs a grocery shop.

SALENA With the yellow door?

RAYAH That's the one

SALENA I've like totally been there!

RAYAH No. Way. I used to work there weekends.

SALENA There was a man in there with like a crazy smile. Like four teeth or sumin. That your dad?

RAYAH Yeh bruv that's my dad! FYI he's got five teeth.

SALENA We should like totally meet up and chat Zayn yo.

RAYAH That would be awesome bruv but I'm not in London anymore. Moved out a few months back.

SOSA i burst out into the cold wet dirty air of brixton high street

    i'm rolling past roxy and up the hill and
    shit
    i'm empty handed

    eva's gonna be pissed at me if i don't represent
    and i refuse to be present
    at this party sober

    so i turn on my heels
    to the one-stop shop two streets down

i see it in the distance

bright neon lights glowing in the night

and yellow door with peeling posters

of national lottery and oyster card info

in i go

and the computer bell ding dings my entrance

head up straight to the wine like i'm old enough to drink it

and take a moment to peruse the vintage

3.99 looks the cheapest

but it looks nasty

fuck that.

i pick up the 4.99 and turn to the till

and then i see her

SIMON I'm streaming dreams,

and something is thumping

inside my head.

I shake awake and realise I'm in bed,

and it's my phone buzzing and jumping;

why's someone messaging me this early man?

I roll over and reach,

tip the screen

towards my eyes,

and go blind

as phone light hits eye.

I squint. Try to catch a hint

of what's going on through tightly shut eyelids.

Why is she messaging me?

I scroll and read.

EVA *speaks directly to* **SIMON**. *He doesn't respond.*

EVA Simon WTF

Those messages were private exclamation

WTF have you done question

Listen I know you're pissed off with me but this is not OK

Simon seriously exclamation exclamation

You don't have to talk to me but please take those pictures down

What if my dad sees question

How could you do this to me question

You fucking bastard

You pathetic ugly small cocked bastard

Can't believe I was ever with a waste of space immature little boy like you

Rob is so much better that you ever were

Simon comma please comma I'm sorry comma I am comma I really am

Please just take the pictures down

I'm sorry for what I said but what if my dad sees question

You know what he's like

How am I meant to go to college this morning exclamation

Simon call me exclamation exclamation exclamation exclamation exclamation

SIMON What she on about?

I don't reply.

I go straight to Facebook to take a look.

Oh my fucking god.
Shit!

A laugh starts from my lips,
and bursts out into the darkness of my room.

Then my stomach sinks.

Everyone's going to think I did this.

SALENA Yo Rayah. I've been looking through your tweets. Girl, are you in Syria?

RAYAH Hey Salena. Yeh I am. I'm in Islamic State Territory. How's things with you?

SALENA Oh my god that's like crazy. You're there right now?

RAYAH Uh yeh!

SALENA That's so weird. Hi! Salam sis! How long you been there?

RAYAH Like four months.

SALENA How come?

RAYAH "O Muslims in all places. Who so is able to emigrate to the Islamic State, let him emigrate. For emigration to the Abode of Islam is obligatory."

SALENA What's that?

RAYAH Duh it's the call of the Caliphate. You are Muslim right?

SALENA Yeh. But what is it?

RAYAH Sis. It means all true Muslims must come to Islamic State.

SALENA What? Serious?

RAYAH If you're a true Muslim, then yeh.

SALENA But that's crazy bruv!

RAYAH Bruv you playing me?

SALENA What?

RAYAH You're playing me aren't you?

SALENA What do you mean?

RAYAH I thought you were Muslim.

SALENA I am Muslim.

RAYAH You're not.

SALENA Of course I am sis.

RAYAH Is this a trap? Are you catfishing me?

SALENA What? What you on about?

RAYAH You said it was crazy.

SALENA What?

RAYAH You just said listening to Allah's call is crazy.

SALENA No all I meant was –

RAYAH How can you be a true Muslim and say that?

SALENA I'm sorry I –

RAYAH My faith is the most important thing to me Salena. I don't want to talk about it with people who don't feel the same.

SALENA But I do feel the same. I love Allah. Of course I do. I'm sorry. I didn't mean to upset you. I really didn't.

RAYAH That's ok. I forgive you.

SOSA she's there
    in the flesh

i'm not messing
tall and lean and slick and
just
i am seriously stressing

her voice is in my ears
but she's here
buying smokes and making jokes with boss man
behind the till

shit

what do I say

i know her in her screen
i know her as a sound that beams
she's in my daylight and my nightlight dreams

but now she's here
in real life
like a 3D movie just for me

wait

what the fuck is she doing here?
this is south

this ain't her ground

i peek round the heinz
as she flicks her hood off
that shaved black head
and see that dark tattoo blue on the back of her neck

fuck me she's even more beautiful in real life

i've been twisting my hands so tight
round the neck of this white
that the screw top cap pops loose

i take a swig of the juice

i think i'll be all cool and chill and be like
hey you're that rapper with the tunes on the internet
Mak
MakDown yeh
i think i've heard of you

but as the wine slips down i see her frown and i realise i've
just said without any introduction

"I'm completely in love with you."

fuck

maybe i can just run

but there's a half drunk bottle of wine in my hand and
MakDown's holding her ground as her soft slim sinewy frame
peng
so peng
is wide in my way

i
want
to
die

she looks at me

"You like my music yeh?"

i try to look cool
though i'm clearly some fan girl fool

"I'm streaming you right now."

i take out my ears and hold one up for her to hear

i see a glint of pride as her own voice enters her mind

"What's your name?"

"Esosa," i tell her, "I know it's lame."

"God's child," she says, "I like it. Good name for a song."

i go weak at the knees

"Hey. You're not the one with the cool posts?
Sosghost?
Or sumin like that?"

she reads my comments

then she says

"Your comments are sick. Like really great. Make me feel
like a proper rap star, like
Queen MakD.
The bee's knees."

my knees that were weak start to shake and break

"I grew up near you and it speaks to me you know."

and her smile gets wider

"No way. You from my endz?"

and we start to chat about streets and beats
dark cuts and corners of the estate
and where we never go when it's late

and she even mentions that park
the park
and which crew lives where
and which of her mates has gone to a better place
and i tell her my sister would be 15 now if only i'd leant her
my bike that night

and time just stands still
as we fill this one stop shop with our childhood lives

SIMON Was it you question

JC What question

  What you waking me for question

SIMON Was it you question

JC What question exclamation

SIMON Facebook

JC What about it

SIMON You seen Facebook

JC Nah

  Why question

SIMON Go on

JC What

SIMON Go on fullstop

JC Dot dot dot

Hold on

BRB

EVA As the world wakes and morning comes,

I hear my dad downstairs eating breakfast buns.

I'm tight and twisted ducked in duvet,

I listen as he leaves for the day.

Simon hasn't replied to a single message or call.

The bastard's ignoring me.

And all this time I feel this fear and this rage,

as more and more disgusting comments appear on the page,

then the vomit springs up again.

JC Laughing crying face

LOL this is hilarious exclamation

Have you seen the comments exclamation question

SIMON Yup fullstop

JC Laughing face laughing face laughing face

Well done man

Serves her right

Wink

SIMON Mate it wasn't me

JC Question

SIMON I didn't do it exclamation

JC Question question question

SIMON I didn't do it exclamation

It wasn't me exclamation

JC Who was it then question

SIMON Andy question question

    Who else had the photos question question

JC Hahahahahahahaha exclamation exclamation exclamation

    I knew he was a legend Muscle emoji Thumbs up emoji

    Rob's going to be well pissed off Angry face

    His new girlfriend's pussy is all over the fucking internet exclamation Sad cat

    Laughing crying face

SIMON This is not funny

    Seriously

JC Wink

    Pretty funny to me

SALENA *(alone)*

    Beneath my single duvet sheet
    his face glows golden in the weak
    light of the moon.

    The poster looms with his bright white teeth,
    beneath golden brown skin and a twinkle in his eye,
    and I imagine that I am
    the luckiest girl in the world
    and he has just proposed to me.

    He sings

    and gives me a shining ring.

    The way his black opal eyes will look into mine as we repeat
    the ijab and qabool,
    to a room full of our families and friends

glowing like stars

as we sign the akad nikah;

and they cheer

and Allah will bless us.

I want my wedding to be magical.

RAYAH That was just what my wedding was like.

SALENA You're married?

RAYAH I am Ukhti. I married a sincere brother after making Hijrah to al-Raqqa. I can't believe how much Allah has blessed me since coming here. My husband is so brave and strong and handsome.

SALENA Can't believe you're married. How old are you?

RAYAH Sixteen. But I was fifteen when I made Hijrah.

SALENA Sister! I'm sixteen too!

RAYAH I know you fool! We started chatting on your birthday!

SALENA Duh! Totally forgot. Can't believe how long we've been chatting.

RAYAH I know right! I feel like you're my sister. Really want to meet you in person!

SALENA I know me too! I'm so jealous Ukhti. I'd love to get married. I'm totally ready.

RAYAH Just say the word sis and I can hook you up.

SALENA Haha thanks!

RAYAH I'm being serious sis. There are so many brothers here who'd jump at the chance to have a wife like you.

SALENA Haha thanks but I'll have to pass.

RAYAH Why? I don't understand you Salena. You say you want something and then when someone offers it to you you refuse it. Maybe you're just not mature enough to get married.

SALENA I am mature. I am. I'd love to get married. But it's impossible.

RAYAH Impossible? Salena when will you realise? With Allah's guidance you can do anything you wish.

SOSA we start to wander towards the door still back and forthing

when the man behind the till

stops me dead

"You paying for that? How old are you?"

i mutter and fumble and reach for my fake id

MakD sees

and says

"Hey let me get that for you. Least I can do for a fan."

she smiles at me and flashes her lashes

in a way that crashes

smashes my whole soul apart

we leave and begin to walk the hill

passing the wine between us like long time brederin

we pass a group of hooded girls and boys

hugging shadows

quick as sparrows

one of them says something to us

CHORUS what's this north London ting doing in our endz

SOSA but we don't acknowledge

we're in a different world to them

she tells me she's writing something new
something different

and from the back pocket of her deep black skinks
she gets out a small black notebook with small black inks
and on the black pavement of this black night
between warping wires of electricity
she starts to rap
straight to me
the most beautiful poetry

it's about her bro that died
it's everything she feels inside
and about how she wants to be who she is
not hide or apologise and not give a shit

and all those things that i just can't like can't begin to say
are right there in front of me
floating from her soft red lips

she talks about the loss and the grief of losing someone
you love
and the hell of the streets and that we should trust in God
above
and the lyrics just stroke me and pierce me with soft sharp
blows
and her final words at her poetry close goes

"The cookies in my heart
Have left your trail behind.
And I can't stop missing;
I can't stop missing;
I won't stop missing you."

the rest of the street has melted like plastic beneath our feet

and we are the only two beings in the world

SIMON My phone won't stop beeping, with people in school
either telling me I'm a legend or a fool.

I run out of energy typing
"It wasn't me. Sort out your facts."
And it's annoying because Andy won't text me back.
The fucking twat.
Beep. Another message. Shit it's from Rob. I read:

"You little piece of shit
I am going to shank you
Watch your back."

Then JC is texting me.

JC Hey Si comma

Just letting you know Rob's heard and he's on the warpath
fullstop

He's planning to shank you after business studies Knife
Explosion

SIMON Thanks mate fullstop

Yeh he's messaged me abuse

JC You spoken to Andy

SIMON Nah

Airing me fullstop

JC Bastard

You seen Eva question

SIMON Not come in today eek face

JC　Ha

　　Don't blame her

　　Now everyone knows she wears a push up

　　Wink Bikini

SIMON　Lol I could have told you that

JC　Lol

SIMON　Loool

JC　Looooooooooooooool

SIMON　Loooooooooooooooooooooooooooooooooooooooool

JC　What you gonna do about Rob question

SIMON　Shrug

JC　I got your back man

　　Hundred percent

　　Muscles

　　Ninja

　　Crossed swords

SIMON　Thanks

　　Think I'll skip business

JC　Wise kemosabe

　　It's Ramadan right question

　　Maybe that's why he's MIA question

SIMON　Dude he can still text exclamation

JC　Oh fullstop

　　Then he's just airing you fullstop

SIMON　Shit wish you'd never told me about Shanna's party

JC　Salena's the one who told everyone

　　You seen her question

SIMON No

JC Think she's gone into hiding doesn't want the blow back

SIMON See you on CoD later question

JC Thumbs up

SOSA suddenly in the stillness i hear the smack smack of rubber on paving

Some of the **CHORUS** *enter.*

SALENA Salam Rayah. Subhanallah. Have you heard?

SOSA hoods surround us

SIMON Rob's boys surround me

SALENA Sister there's been an attack.

SOSA there's a cry and a shout

SIMON I hear him shout.

> **ROB** *to* **SIMON.**

CHORUS Simon, you little piece of shit

The **CHORUS** *surround* **SIMON.** **ROB** *steps out and towers above him. Some of the* **CHORUS** *get out their mobile phones and stand filming as* **ROB** *punches* **SIMON** *several times, knocks him to the ground and kicks him.* **SIMON** *goes still.* **ROB** *moves away. The* **CHORUS** *put away their mobile phones.*

SOSA and then the hoods turn and leave screaming and whooping into the night

and then it's just me and MD again back in our silence

her eyes are down

SIMON I drag myself up from the ground,

My ears playing this piercing sound,

Everything cracks and everything aches as I shake the caked dirt off me.

My head is screaming, and my nose is streaming blood. I go to touch it and the whole bone shifts,

And this shooting pain rips through my sinuses.

Fuck I think it's broken.

SOSA i follow her gaze and see her arms clasped tight across stomach

and in the light of the street lamps i see

this silver black liquid start to flow through fingers

flowing and flowing

and she's trying to stop it and it won't

she looks up at me

her eyes wide

her mouth silent

she coughs

and the same black liquid spatters out through her teeth staining white to black and red

she falls to her knees

SALENA On the BBC screen
    I watch sombre reporters
    all hustling and bustling
    round police tape and cordons.
    Mothers and daughters,
    friends out for the night,
    their eyes bright
    from the blue flashing lights
    and the world in turmoil.

    Eye-witness interviews and birds-eye-views.
    And victims
    hugged in tin foil
    on the street side.

    They show the videos people took,
    as the area shook
    in the moment of attack.
    They pan over the rubble,
    and say the trouble is
    they don't yet know how many might have died.
    The death count may rise.

    And I think of the waste of life; the pointless futility.

    Islamic State have taken responsibility.

SIMON Eva fullstop
    Your boyfriend broke my fucking nose

SALENA How could anyone do that?

EVA Oh now you reply

ANDY Alright dude

Just seen your messages dot dot dot

SIMON *(to ANDY)* Andy exclamation

Where the fuck you been man question exclamation

EVA Take those pictures down or I'll get Rob to break something else fullstop

ANDY Sorry man

Not a good day

No data and I'm starving

What's up

SIMON *(to EVA)* I've not done nothing

(to ANDY) I need you to take it down

EVA You put naked pictures of me on the internet exclamation exclamation

ANDY Question

EVA Exclamation exclamation

SIMON *(to ANDY)* The profile

EVA Exclamation

ANDY You've lost me dot dot question

SIMON *(to EVA)* It wasn't me

EVA Bullshit fullstop

You're the only one who had them fullstop

SIMON *(to EVA)* You cheated on me remember

EVA So you're getting me back question

SIMON *(to* EVA*)* I'm just saying

 (to ANDY*)* Seriously Andy

 Be a mate

EVA WTF question exclamation

SIMON *(to* ANDY*)* It was funny and everything but I've had the crap beaten out of me fullstop

 I'm in A&E Eva's messaging me being a bitch fullstop

 I need you to take down the Facebook profile

ANDY Of what question

SIMON *(to* ANDY*)* Caps lock EVA

EVA I know I cheated but that doesn't mean you can do this

ANDY Question

 I didn't make a facebook profile of Eva dot dot dot

 What is it question

SIMON *(to* ANDY*)* Insert link

 (to EVA*)* I didn't do this to you exclamation

ANDY Shit

 That's hilarious

SIMON *(to* ANDY*)* So it wasn't you question

ANDY Nah mate

 I'm being a good Muslim boy aren't I exclamation

EVA Stop lying exclamation

 Least I don't have to fake it with Rob

SIMON *(to* EVA*)* Fuck you

 Enjoy your porn career

ANDY I may have sent a few to Mike dot dot dot

EVA Wait

ANDY And Tibs dot dot dot

EVA Please fullstop

ANDY And Leo eek face

EVA Please take them down

SIMON *(to* **ANDY***)* Shit

    Andy

    WTF exclamation

    (to **EVA***)* Why should I question

ANDY What question

EVA I'm literally begging you fullstop

    My anxiety is going bad again and you know what I'm like dot dot dot

    What if my dad sees question

    I know I hurt you but please comma this won't make anything better fullstop

    Please fullstop

SIMON *(to* **ANDY***)* Eva's gonna kill me

ANDY Sorry man

    You should've said

SIMON *(to* **ANDY***)* No it's ok fullstop

    Just try and find out will you

    Save me getting another beating

ANDY Sure

SIMON *(to* **ANDY***)* Let me know asap question

ANDY Thumbs up

    ANDY *disappears.*

SIMON I'm sorry Eva but it really wasn't me

EVA You were the only one who had them

SIMON I may have shown them to some of the lads dot dot dot

EVA Caps lock WTF

> **ANDY** *reappears.*

ANDY FYI Just seen the vid of Rob beating you to a pulp

Making a remix exclamation

Gonna be hilarious exclamation

SIMON *(to* EVA*)* Fuck you you bastard fullstop

EVA What question exclamation exclamation

SIMON *(to* EVA*)* Shit

Sorry

That wasn't meant for you

EVA Who are you talking to question

SIMON *(to* EVA*)* None of your business

EVA Grow up

You need to fix this

SIMON *(to* EVA*)* I'll see what I can do dot dot dot

SALENA Rayah. Rayah. Do you get UK news? Have you heard what's happened here?

EVA Ok

Thank you fullstop

Smile emoji

SALENA Sister there's been a terrorist attack. Nine people have died, maybe more.

RAYAH Salam. He was not a terrorist Ukhti. He was a true believer and soldier of the Islamic State.

SALENA What? Rayah. He was a terrorist.

RAYAH I used to think like you, but look at the bigger picture Salena. Many many more of our people died in those strikes against Mosul. They murder us, they drop bombs on our homes. They do not call those a terrorist attack.

SALENA That doesn't mean it's ok.

RAYAH When will you realise we're at war Ukhti? No one wants to kill but think about it; white men with tanks and aeroplanes and machine guns who can wipe out entire cities of Muslims are called soldiers. They're called brave Ukhti. It's only true Muslims with nothing but their faith to protect them who are called terrorists. So many of our people have been tragically killed. How can you stand it?

SALENA But those people were innocent.

RAYAH So were the people of Mosul.

SALENA But it's different it's –

RAYAH How.

SALENA It just is.

RAYAH I don't think we should talk any more.

SALENA What? Why?

RAYAH Why don't you actually read the Qu'ran Salena. If you want to have a proper conversation with me let me know. But I have no interest in talking to an ignorant western girl about something as important as the preservation of Islam. It's insulting to me. It's insulting to our faith. And it is insulting to Allah.

SALENA But –

RAYAH ma'aasalaama.

SALENA But Rayah. Who else do I have to talk to about this?

SOSA i press my hands against her belly but i can't plug the leak

RAYAH You have Allah.

SOSA i can't stop the blood flowing and flowing out of her out
of her
and soon it's dyed her hoodie and her jeans
and in the distance i still hear those screams

then we're not alone

white lights of mobile phones
and screens

and i can't believe my eyes

they're just standing there
not helping

filming her here
dying and crying on the brixton pavement

and the blood that bubbles out of her
bubbles into my cheeks
as this rage inside starts to explode out of me

"What the fuck you doing you sick fucks. She's dying. Help
her she's dying."

the white flashing lights turn to blue
but they can't get through
because there are too
many phones in the way
wanting a good view

EVA The next 48 hours pass in a daze.
   I sit in a haze of hollowness and rage.
   My phone never stops.
   I throw it against the wall and it smashes and drops
   into trousers and tops.

   I was meant to post a new vid last night,
   but I couldn't bring myself to dress or to fight.

   When dad asks me what's wrong
   I say it's some kind of bug.
   He gives me a hug.

   It feels like a punch straight in my gut.

   It's been 3 days and my nudes are still up.
   What the fuck?

   I message Simon but he's not replying.
   Neither's Rob.
   I've not heard from him since he heard I'd been exposed
   and broke Simon's nose.
   I want him here to say it will be ok.
   I feel like an animal trapped in a cage
   there are hundreds more comments since yesterday.
   I look away.
   I can't bear it.

   I decide to ignore,
   withdraw from the outpour
   of perverts and abuse, of boyfriends and exes,
   and fake concerned text-es
   from people pretending they care.

I put on some music.

and try to forget.

She begins to dance.

The **CHORUS** *enter and move around her.*

CHORUS Hey Eva lovers look at this. Insert jpeg

Great dancer's body What else can you do with it

Hey Eva fans look what Eva's doing

She's got some moves

I'd dance with Eva

I'd do more than dance

She loves it

Dirty slut

My mate owns this club he's looking for girls with talent

You could make a fortune Give him a call 020746830178

Stay sexy babe wink

ANDY *re-enters.*

ANDY JC exclamation

Check out the remix I've made of Simon's fight fullstop insert link

JC OMG laughing face

Our poor boy

Forward

Share

The moment when **SIMON** *is beaten up is repeated to music by the* **CHORUS**. *It spreads exponentially as each person sends it to someone else so there are many* **SIMON**s *being beaten up to the music, all identical. They can freeze and rewind and replay.*

Some people comment on **EVA**. *Others comment on*
SIMON. *The dialogue can be interwoven so both comment*
threads are happening simultaneously.

CHORUS *(comments to* **SIMON***)* Haha that guys a total pussy

Hey man look at this #firstruleoffightclub

Dude He doesn't even try to fight back

Hey look at this Trending on twitter #hilarious

Check out this remix

CHORUS *(comments to* **EVA***)* Oh my god these pics are disgusting
I used to really love Eva but now

I know I can't believe she'd do that What a whore Not going
to watch her videos any more

Nor me

Me either Can't believe it Urgh

I'll watch her Over and over again

And me

The **CHORUS** *disappear leaving* **EVA** *alone, dancing.*

An unknown **VOICE**, *different from the others...*

VOICE Hi Eva

How are you today

I saw your nudes

You must be so embarrassed

I would be

You're clearly gagging for it

EVA *(to the* **VOICE***)* Who are you question

How'd you get this number question

VOICE Hahahahahahaha

SALENA Salam Rayah. I know you're not talking to me but I wanted to tell you I've been reading. Trying to learn more about Islam.

EVA Leave me alone

VOICE Hahahahahaha

SALENA I tried talking to my friends but they just keep trying to drag me in to their stupid dramas. No one is listening to me and it's driving me crazy. I'm going to request to speak to the Imam so he can answer some of my questions.

SOSA i'm bloodsoaked and crying outside the emergency room

SALENA Anyway, wanted to let you know I'm trying to be a better Muslim. Sorry if I upset you.

SOSA my phone beeps

"Have you heard? MD's dead. Taken down by the Brixton crew.

They've posted it on YouTube.

Stabbed 18 times."

18 times

where'd they get that from

i reply
quick

"She's not dead. She's still alive."

one tick

two ticks

two ticks blue

and my girl's responded

RAYAH Salam Salena.

SOSA "She can't be. Look at twitter."

RAYAH I'm glad you're reading but you gotta be careful who you speak to. Many religious leaders in the west are trying to protect the infidels – your Imam may be one of them. I'm also worried about these so-called friends of yours. It sounds like they care more about gossip then they do about you and your faith and the journey that you are on. Think about whether these are the people you want to spend your time with. If you have any questions you can ask me. Any time you like. I'm always here.

VOICE Hi Eva

How are you today

SALENA Thank you Ukhti. That means a lot. Maybe you're right – think I'll keep my distance from all them for a bit. Thank you so much for your advice. I don't know what I'd do without you.

EVA Who are you question

Leave me alone

VOICE A friend

RAYAH I'm always here for you Ukhti. I really care about you. From now on let's talk on Kik ok? It's more private.

EVA You're not my friend

VOICE I have some friendly advice

EVA What question

VOICE Go kill yourself

EVA Fuck you whoever you are you sad pathetic lonely fuck who's got nothing better than to hide behind a phone you coward exclamation Fuck you fullstop

VOICE Does your dad know you're a whore

EVA I'm not a whore

VOICE Are you sure

Why don't you ask him

EVA What question

VOICE Let's see what his opinion is

EVA What question

VOICE Let's send him some pictures of his sweet

EVA *(to* HERSELF*)* No

VOICE Beautiful

EVA *(to* HERSELF*)* No no

VOICE Innocent

EVA *(to* HERSELF*)* Oh my god

VOICE Whore of daughter

EVA *is distraught.*

EVA No don't please exclamation

VOICE Oh dear

Too late

RAYAH Salam sis. Please don't be angry but I've done something crazy.

EVA *(to* HERSELF*)* Oh my god!

SALENA Salam sister. What is it?

RAYAH So I hope you don't mind but I kind of showed your picture to one of the brothers here. He told me to tell you he thinks you're beautiful.

SALENA Oh my gosh no he didn't!

RAYAH He did. He said you were totally hilwa.

SALENA Oh my gosh sis I'm blushing.

RAYAH Seriously Ukhti. So many brothers said how pretty you are. If you did want a husband you could totally have your pick!

SALENA Oh my gosh what's he like? Is he handsome?

RAYAH Uh yeh. He's like Zayn but taller.

SALENA No he isn't.

RAYAH He is!!

SALENA What does he do?

RAYAH He fights on the frontline with my husband. Most of them do.

SALENA Isn't sixteen a little young to be married?

RAYAH Uh no. Aisha, the Prophet's wife got married when she was nine!

SALENA Yeh but what's it like? Being married and that?

RAYAH Really amazing. I'm so much happier now I'm not in Dar al-Kufr.

SALENA But why?

RAYAH Duh. Because I am closer to Allah. I am fighting for Islam. Look what's happening in America, they don't even want our people to enter the so-called 'land of the free'. Look at Britain at Europe at Russia. The abuse we suffer at the hands of the infidels. They're trying to destroy Islam in any way they can. I can't let that happen. Can you?

SALENA No but –

RAYAH Even in schools now you say the wrong thing and the teacher reports you as an extremist. Why do that unless they want to stamp out our faith? Don't you feel afraid?

SALENA I do. But there are still a lot of Muslims here. I have friends who –

RAYAH Again you talk of these friends Salena. They're not good for you. They don't listen to you or care about you like I do. And even if they did, are you telling me these so-called friends of yours don't feel marginalised? Persecuted because they are Muslim? Don't strangers abuse them on the street?

SALENA It's definitely hard being a Muslim here.

EVA It's the silence that's the worst

RAYAH All I can say Ukhti is I am so much happier now I'm here and closer to God.

EVA He won't even look at me.
    I'm sat on the settee;
    and his eyes are red like there's been tears
    blinked back.
    And we're just sat.

When he does speak his voice is weird,
tight and stretched,
and much quieter than normal.

I've been preparing for the shout,
for the anger that has always just burst out.
That bout of anger and hate
that makes the whole house quake.

But this. This is worse.

This is like our bodies are lying in a hearse
together.
And we cannot sever ourselves from being buried alive
forever.

I don't know what he says to me
but the word 'Disappointed' and 'I brought you up better'.
And then my eyes get wetter
as he tells me I'm deluded,
and how could I be so stupid,
and each word is like a knife in my gut,
and I want to shut him and the world out of everything.

I cry and I cry.

ANDY JC mate I just got a visit from the feds exclamation
Was intense exclamation

EVA God please let me die.

JC Shit fullstop
What happened question

ANDY Eva's Dad called them fullstop

JC and **ANDY** *continue their text conversation.* **SIMON**
speaks to the audience.

SIMON "You little fuck" he's thinking. Blinking
quickly and slickly as he scribbles ink on the form in front
on the scratched plastic of the table top.

"This is so unfair,"
I explain,

"It wasn't my fault."

And his head lifts with a jolt.

JC Caps lock what

SIMON *(to* **AUDIENCE***)* I can feel my mum stock still in the
chair to my left. She's trying not to move or say anything.

My stomach is in my chest,
my heart is pressed
into my intestines.
This is the worst.

"You have to understand Simon,"

He rolls Simon round his tongue
like tasteless chewing gum.

"that whatever your intent this is a serious offence."

ANDY I'm in so much trouble fullstop

SIMON *(to* **AUDIENCE***)* "Distribution of child sexual abuse images
cannot be taken lightly."

ANDY It's child porn exclamation

JC Child porn

JC AND SIMON What the Fuck

JC question exclamation

SIMON *(to* **AUDIENCE***)* I can hear my mum suck in the shock.

JC I thought it was about Eva question

SIMON *(to* **AUDIENCE***)* "Eva's 17" I say.

"She's legal."

This is totally insane.

I hate that mum has to be in here with me.

Why couldn't they have spoken to me privately?

I can feel every bit of her disappointment cutting into my skin

outside and within.

It's so fucking mortifying,

I think actually dying

right now would be better

than sat with her hurt

and disappointment

boring down into me.

JC She's 17 exclamation question

ANDY I know exclamation

SIMON *(to* **AUDIENCE***)* But the guy leans forward with a kindly yellow smile

that bores

into my pores

like a metal file:

ANDY Apparently any nudes of under 18s is child porn Eye roll

SIMON *(to* **AUDIENCE***)* "I'm afraid under the law, possessing an indecent photograph of a child is an offence."

JC Bullshit fullstop

SIMON *(to* AUDIENCE*)* "And distribution of those images is a serious offence"

JC It's not like we're fucking peados exclamation

SIMON *(to* AUDIENCE*)* The room is intense,

ANDY I know right

SIMON *(to* AUDIENCE*)* But none of this makes sense.

JC She made those nudes herself

SIMON *(to* AUDIENCE*)* Eva took those photos herself and sent them to me.

So how can it be child pornography?

JC So what they say

SIMON *(to* AUDIENCE*)* "You distributed them to your friends did you not?"

"Just a couple of mates,"

I return like a shot,

"And I didn't ask her to send them to me.

I didn't put the pictures up.

"The Facebook profile has nothing to do with me.

Plus I'm not the one texting her.

I didn't make it create it or put them up on the net.

It was just between mates,

When I was upset."

"When you were upset?"

He jumps at the word.

"So you intended to hurt her?"

ANDY They said we could go to jail dot dot dot

SIMON *(to* AUDIENCE*)* This is fucking absurd!

JC For what question question

ANDY Child porn man exclamation

Plus coz Simon is her ex there's this crime about revenge porn he could be done for as well dot dot dot

JC Fuck

You serious question

ANDY And she's been getting like these nasty texts

They sent the nudes to her dad

JC Who text her question

ANDY Dunno

Anonymous email account

They coming to see you yeh

JC Yeh

ANDY Least they've taken the nudes down from Facebook

JC But they don't know who it was question

ANDY They said they didn't know yet but they've got Facebook on it so they can find out the IP address or something

JC I didn't know they could do that

ANDY I know

Good innit

What your parents said question

JC question.

JC Nothing yet

Might try to keep them out the way

ANDY Can't mate

They have to be in room with you

It's rough

SIMON *(to* **AUDIENCE***)* Once the officer has gone the lectures
begin

JC Fuck

Fuck

SIMON *(to* **AUDIENCE***)* My mum is in tears and my dad's lips
are thin

and pressed tight.

He seems disgusted by the sight

of me.

My nose is still weeping

and burns like a fucking volcano.

People are laughing at me all over the web

watching and rewatching my face get reaarranged;

everything is wrong and strange,

I'm filled with this rage.

But that just spurs another lecture

about how I've ruined my life and ruined my future.

It's like I'm at war as this outpour of attacks

is gunfire I can't hold back.

SOSA i'm on twitter

hashtag MakDown

SIMON *(to* **AUDIENCE***)* This shit has got real

SOSA and all I can see

are hundreds of posts saying

CHORUS RIP

    RIP

    RIP

SOSA there's even an obituary

    and people are quoting her songs

    and on her channel people are posting like it's her tomb

    and the south london crew

    have already uploaded a new vid

    announcing their victory

    announcing the death of MD

    and there's more just

CHORUS RIP

    RIP

    RIP

SOSA and then some sick fuck saying

CHORUS Good riddance to the fucking bitch

    I always thought she was a piece of shit

SOSA and then there's a link

    and i click without thinking

    and suddenly i'm blinking

    watching myself holding MD's body beneath the crowds
    and street-lamps

    as she lies in her own blood on the hill

    i shout in a voice that isn't my own

CHORUS What the fuck are you doing you sick fucks?

SOSA i'm there on the street and
    my screaming and MakD bleeding
    is put on repeat like some scratched disc

    over and over again

    and underneath people are aksing

CHORUS Who's that bitch with her
    She's got a mouth on her
    Calm down love
    Look at what she's wearing
    Nasty ho

SOSA that wine is spinning round my head and all i can type is
    she ain't dead
    there's still hope
    save your RIPs
    she's alive
    in A&E
    listen to me please

    but all i get back is flak

CHORUS What do you know? That skank is dead

SOSA no she ain't she's in a hospital bed

    then suddenly before i know
    i get another message

CHORUS Hey are you that ho from the video?

SOSA i immediately block but the damage is done

CHORUS Are you her girlfriend

    Dirty lezzer

    Scissor sister

    Carpet muncher

    Dyke

    Disgusting

    Unnatural

    Dirty pervert

SOSA and all those ugly words that people throw

    if you don't fit the fucking sexual status quo

    it hurts

    it fucking

SALENA I'm walking home,

    checking my phone.

SOSA my followers go up and i'm being questioned and quizzed
and slagged off and tagged

    this has got real bad real quick

SALENA Nike Airs smack against tarmac;

    head down,

    shoulders slack,

    handbag –

    coz Muslims

    can't wear backpacks

    without getting looks.

People look at me warily;
it used to be occasionally,
now it's all the time.

My news alert chimes.

Oh my gosh.

There's been another attack.
This time on Muslim's at prayer,
there's blood and people everywhere,
most faces are scared.

I go straight to twitter to get the down low,
check there's no one there that I know
and to see what happened and what people are saying.

And beneath pictures of victims and people praying
this is what I read:

CHORUS #whatgoesaroundcomesaround Now they know how
we feel

About time someone fought back against terrorists
#justiceforUK #bloodforblood

If we #banislam now millions of lives will be saved
#islamisevil #eatmorebacon

Acid may have burnt off skin, but not the terrorism in their
hearts #notfarenough

They got what they derverve #banislam #religionofpiss

And my gut fills with hate.

JC *reappears.*

JC *(to* ANDY*)* This is bullshit exclamation

SALENA   It stretches and tightens inside me.

JC   If she didn't want anyone to see those nudes she shouldn't have sent them in the first place

SALENA   Rayah was right. London is Jahannam. And I am living in it.

ANDY   That what they say question

JC   Fucking pigs exclamation

Pig emoji

You shouldn't have put them up man

ANDY   Fuck off

You were the one who sent them to me in the first place

JC   No it wasn't

Why you lying about me question

ANDY   You're the one who's lying exclamation

JC   Don't go lying to the police about me I done nothing

ANDY   It was you mate Si sent me nothing dot dot dot

JC   JC is typing

JC is typing

JC was last seen at 23:08

SALENA   How would I even get there?

RAYAH Oh my gosh Ukhti it's so easy. I'll send you instructions.

SALENA Can you send me a picture of him?

RAYAH I'd love to but it's too dangerous.

SALENA Ok I'll let you know if I decide to come.

RAYAH The day of judgement is near Ukhti. He's exactly like
       Zayn I promise. Don't you trust me?

SALENA I do, it's just –

RAYAH It's OK to be scared. But seriously it's far more dangerous
       where you are now. Think of all those Muslims they just
       attacked. What if it's your mosque next? Remember what
       Allah says in the Qu'ran: "Do not be afraid. I am with you,
       all hearing all seeing."

SALENA Alhamdulilah. I'd miss Shanna the most.

RAYAH Of course you'll miss her!

SOSA there's even a gif of her down on the ground

RAYAH But once you're here you could help her to make Hijrah
       and if she's a friend and true Muslim she will come and
       then you'd be reunited.

SOSA when her spine goes stiff

      and her eyes start to drift

SALENA That would be amazing.

SOSA #anotherlesbianbitesthedust

      and memes of her like jesus on the cross

crying emoji

sorry for your loss

and others saying

she's overrated

or

the best rapper god ever created

and the homophobic hate still fills up my feed
whilst her lyrics are tweeted and the retweets increase
and every fucker in the world is trying to get a piece
of the fucking action
and

#makdownssmakdown

gets traction
and now bbc news have the story
and there's a new update with all the gory details
and then they dm me and aks for a comment

EVA I've not left the house,
and I've not washed in a week.

SOSA i can't take these words any more

The **CHORUS** *turn on* **EVA.**

CHORUS Nice tits Eva

Hun wtf r u ok

Wot a slag

SOSA i'm drowning in the voices of a thousand strangers

EVA I can barely think and I cannot sleep.

SOSA and my lungs and my brain are just swimming in lies
that I can't stop breathing in

VOICE Hi Eva

CHORUS I'd smash that

Lmfao

Too skinny for me

VOICE Where have all your nudes gone

Don't worry

I've put them on this site

CHORUS Fat bitch

Hahahahahahahahaha

Tiny tits

Hahahahahahahahaha

EVA The texts keep coming one by one.

CHORUS Hear no evil speak no evil see no evil monkeys

EVA Kill yourself kill yourself.

Just do it go on.

VOICE And this one

EVA I still don't know who they come from
but I'm starting to think that—

CHORUS Eye heart emoji Tongue emoji

VOICE And this

CHORUS Aubergine emoji water droplets emoji

VOICE And this

EVA I'm on porn sites everywhere.
And for each that's deleted another appears.

VOICE I wouldn't try to find me if I were you
Bad things could happen

CHORUS Slut slut slut slut slut slut heart lick heart lick
Hahaha

EVA I can't go online, I can't check my phone,
I can't go to college,
I'm completely alone.
My dance career has been ruined forever,
And if I can't dance,

CHORUS Kill yourself

VOICE Just kill yourself

CHORUS Go kill yourself

EVA If I can't dance

VOICE Go on Eva

EVA *and the* **CHORUS** *disappear.*

SALENA OK! This is happening! I can't believe it!

RAYAH I'm so excited Ukhti!

SALENA I'm bringing my Zayn poster with me. Can't wait to show you it. It's proper massive.

RAYAH Aw I would love to see it but I think it's best you leave it behind.

SALENA Oh. How come?

RAYAH Sis, it won't be allowed.

SALENA Oh my gosh I'm being stupid aren't I?

RAYAH It's totally ok. It gets so much easier once you're here. When you're with your brothers and sisters sharing in the glory of Allah you'll realise you just don't need western idols. And you'll have your own Zayn soon. He's so excited to meet you!

SALENA It's starting to feel real now. Rayah, what if he doesn't like me?

RAYAH What? You're beautiful Salena!

SALENA For real. This is like a massive deal. What if I don't like it there? What if I don't like him?

RAYAH You will love it here I promise. And I will be here to help you in your new life. We'll be together Ukhti! I'm so excited to see you.

SOSA hours later i'm woken by a face and told to follow

my back's bent by plastic

i'm exhausted and hollow

SALENA I'm excited about seeing you too.

But Rayah are you sure?

RAYAH Have faith sister.

Everything is arranged.

It's too late to change things now.
I'll see you when you arrive in Dawla.

SOSA and then she's there
in the flesh

SALENA See you soon inshallah.

SOSA deep dark brown limbs with white bright plastic tube
coming from upturned arms deep dark brown skull and
deep dark black hair on white bright starch and bright
white blanket tucked up beneath elbows with hardly a crease

her lip curls at one edge a half faced smile and i hover
not sure what to do

"god's child"
says the smile
no voice all air

EVA I wake up in a hospital bed.

SOSA and my heart lifts like a helium balloon

EVA The lights are too bright and my eyelids too red.
My dad's in a corner of the room.
My body is filled with plastic and tubes
and there's a repetitive beep by my head.

ANDY Mate have you heard question

SIMON Yeh

My heads gone

Can't believe she'd do that to herself fullstop

EVA I don't feel relief.

How dare they?

They had no right.

No fucking right.

VOICE Hi Eva

Nice try

Take more pills next time

EVA I want to claw and to bite,

but I'm held back by tubes and this thumping ache

all over my body.

ANDY No man comma not about Eva fullstop

Although that's fucked up

I mean about JC

EVA I want to be dead.

Instead I'm in bed with limbs like lead and a screaming head.

SIMON What about JC question

ANDY *and* **JC** *exit.*

SALENA This is it.

The day.

I'm on my way.

EVA And the knowledge that absolutely nothing has changed.

SALENA Passport packed

old cracked suitcase stacked

with backpack

under feet of the cold bus seat.

We were crushed in:

beans in a tin.

Men with beer and ladies with prams

all squished together;

but they stay away from me.

My family think I'm staying at Shanna's tonight

but really I'm getting my flight.

And by the time it's morning

I'll be soaring

engines roaring

no warning.

EVA I'm there for a week.

Mostly asleep,

with shadows flitting, sitting, whispering, ticking

on charts and checking my heart.

SALENA What if I get caught?

Stopped and searched at the airport?

I push the thought

to the back of my brain.

EVA Dad speaks to me once,

only to say that the police have found the culprit

so there'll be no more texts.

And the pictures have been taken down.
I ask who but he won't tell,

he says I should concentrate on getting well.

SALENA As I sit,
    and watch the neon lit
    streets flit
    by in a blur,
    I think

    "am I doing the right thing?"

    But then this white lad,
    who thinks he is bad
    comes and whispers right in my ear,

    "You dirty Paki."

    And then loud and proud,

CHORUS "Go back to where you're from."

SALENA and then disappears as the bus doors close
    and the wheels turn on.

    The bus is hush and no one says anything
    but they all heard.

    I chew the words
    'go back to where you're from'
    over in my brain.
    Each syllable feels like sharp hard rain,

and I think I am!

I am going to where I belong.

In a few hours I'll be gone

from this godless,

soulless,

hate-filled throng.

SIMON Hey Eva fullstop

I wanted to call but don't know if you've blocked me or changed your number and no one will tell me where you've moved to so I'm just hoping you still check this email account question

SALENA But then to my surprise

SIMON I wanted to say how sorry I am fullstop

SALENA this girl suddenly sits quick

in the space now next to me

SIMON I promise I didn't know it was JC who put them up fullstop

SALENA My heart jumps a beat

as she sits down soft on the dirt clogged seat;

and I'm ready to jump to my feet

if she starts anything.

SIMON And those sick messages he was sending you as well comma I can't believe he did that to you exclamation

I didn't know fullstop

He said it wasn't him fullstop

SALENA White strings lead from her ear drums to back jean pocket,

and heavy gold

swings from each lobe,

with lips painted bright.

SIMON It's ok if you don't forgive me but I hope things are better now wherever you are fullstop

I'm just so fucking glad your dad found you in time and that you're still alive fullstop

SALENA She's clearly off out tonight

SIMON You probably heard I've been expelled question

I'm sorry fullstop

I really am fullstop

Not just for you having to move and what you went through comma but for DancewithEva fullstop

I know how important that was to you fullstop

SALENA slowly she reaches to her ear

SIMON Anyway comma

I'm really sorry Eva

SALENA pulls out the wire

SIMON Simon

    SIMON *exits.*

SALENA and offers it to me.

SOSA *(to* **SALENA***)* You like music blud?

SALENA And she smiles.

    She looks straight into me
    and I take it and wait
    for the floodgate
    of sound to enter my head,
    and something unsaid
    passes between her and me on that bus 333.

    Music plays.

    The music I don't know.

    But it's a girl rapping.

    At first it feels angry and hard like all the other rappers
    of the west
    celebrating anger and sex.

    But then the sea of words separate and clarify.

SOSA for the next hour we talk

    not like we're here in sterile and synth
    but as if
    we're still walking up that same hill

a bottle of wine mixing our dna
and finger prints

and i tell her about the words hurled and unfurled
against me and her
the insults and the hate
and i tell her that twitter's alive with the fact that she's died
and she just rolls her eyes
and says

"shanks and stones may bleed my bones
But your words will make me stronger"

RAYAH Hi Salena, is everything ok?

SALENA I feel her arm pressed up against mine.
and how we are both tied by this one piece of string,
so white and so thin,
linking her mind to mine,
sisters in rhyme.

RAYAH Where are you?

EVA Hi Simon fullstop
Thanks for your message fullstop

RAYAH Why are you not at the meeting point? Did they catch
you?

EVA My new college is ok fullstop

SALENA I don't know how long we sit,

    silently sharing each breath

    and each beat,

    on these two London bus seats.

RAYAH I've been looking at the UK news and it doesn't say anything about anyone being detained. Are you ok?

EVA I've made a few friends comma

    Especially this one girl

    We're off to a party in Brixton tonight exclamation

RAYAH If you got scared that's ok.

EVA I want to tell you I forgive you fullstop

RAYAH Just get in touch and we can talk? Alright? Please.

EVA Please don't contact me again fullstop

SALENA "Sorry I've got to go"

    she suddenly says,

    and I pass back the bud

    and she says

    "Stay strong blud"

    and she's off.

RAYAH Everyone's angry with me. They say I made you up. They say I should be punished. If you don't want me to get in trouble, please get in touch.

EVA I want to be an inspiration,

    for other young women across the nation

    who've had horrible things happen to them.

    I almost lost dancing.

    But this one girl at my new college,

    we've become pretty tight,

    I told her everything that happened

    about the pics and the night

    I downed all those pills.

    And after we've spilled some tears she says to me:

EVA AND SOSA "Don't let people tell you who you are"

SALENA Suddenly I check my twitter feed and see

    That tomorrow hundreds of people

    will line the streets

    where the attacks took place.

    Muslim men and women,

    headscarf to headscarf,

    and hand in hand

    in vigil will stand

    for solidarity, with people of every race,

    faith,

    and creed;

    taking a stand,

    taking a lead.

RAYAH Salena please get in touch

SALENA And all different but the same.

>They'll say,
>#allahislove
>#lovebeatshate.
>
>My anger dissipates.

EVA And then out of the blue

>she takes me to
>a studio
>where people are dancing
>Hip hop. Just a local class.
>And she tells me "girl go shake your ass"
>and I do.
>
>EVA *dances.*

SALENA What was I thinking?

>I wanna be with my friends
>I wanna see them right now.
>I share the link and think
>Maybe Shanna will want to come.
>I DM her
>she messages straight back!
>We make a plan.

EVA It feels amazing.

SOSA suddenly

> the mechanised music of her heart keeping rhythm on the
> monitor behind my head changes time

> the rhythm shifts and the tempo slows

> and steady beats syncopate and freeze becoming one long
> piercing drone

> she's dying help her she's dying

> nurses rush in and i'm pushed away from the bed
> pillows removed from her head
> and electricity is drummed into her body

> and then it's her and me again
> and deep dark brown limbs
> deep dark brown skull
> and deep dark black hair
> on white bright starch
> and bright white blanket
> tucked up beneath elbows with hardly a crease

> but no more tubes
> and no more beat keeping time

RAYAH You are a godless girl.

SOSA shanks and stones
> have bled her bones

RAYAH I see now that you have allied yourself with Shaytan. You will burn in Jahannam for eternity. I pray for Allah's wrath to strike you dead. Burn Salena. Burn with the infidels.

RAYAH *exits.*

SOSA i walk through corridors in a zombie apocalypse
i feel nothing
i hear nothing
nothing except each cardiac beat and pump of my blood
playing silently her words over and over in gapless playback

the cookies in my heart
have left your trail behind

SALENA That night as I ride home

SOSA i can't stop missing

SALENA I look down at my phone

EVA Dancing is me it's who I am

SOSA i can't stop missing

EVA Don't let others stop you

SALENA I know I'm not alone

SOSA i won't stop missing
   you

SOSA, EVA AND SALENA Post.

GLOSSARY OF TERMS

Airing: When a person or multiple people purposely ignore your message on social media

Akad nikah: A written marriage contract for marriage under Islam

Alhamdulillah: An Islamic phrase meaning "praise be to God"

Al-Raqqa: A city in Syria located about 160 km east of Aleppo

Blud: A colloquial term meaning "mate" or "friend"

Caliphate: An area containing an Islamic steward known as a caliph

Catfishing: When someone pretends to be someone they're not using social media to create false identities, particularly to pursue deceptive online romances

CoD: Acronym: Call of Duty (popular first-person shooter video game)

Cookies: A small piece of data sent from a website and stored on the user's computer by the user's web browser while the user is browsing

Dar-al-Kufr: An Arabic phrase meaning "The Land of Non-Believers", i.e. Those who do not believe in Islam

Hijrah: A migration or journey of the Islamic prophet Muhammad and his followers from Mecca to Yathrib, later renamed by him to Medina, in the year 622

Hilwa: An Arabic word meaning "pretty girl"

Hood rat: A derogatory term for a woman seen as promiscuous in her local community

Ijab and qabul: The mutual agreement of bride and groom to marry

Imam: The name of an Islamic leadership position such as a worship leader of a mosque

Inshallah: An Arabic word meaning "God willing"

Jahannam: An Arabic word for the Islamic concept of Hell

Kik: A private messaging app that lets you send encrypted messaging

LMFAO: Acronym: Laughing my fucking ass off

Ma'a Assalama: An Arabic phrase meaning "go without fear"

Meme: An image, video, piece of text, etc typically humorous in nature that is copied and spread rapidly by Internet users, often with variations and captions

Peng: A colloquial term meaning "good looking"

Qur'an: The religious text of Islam

Ramadan: The ninth month of the Islamic calendar, observed by Muslims worldwide as a month of fasting to commemorate the first revelation of the Qur'an to Muhammad

Salam: An Arabic word that means "peace", but also used as a general greeting

Shanking: To stab someone

Sket: slut

Ukhti: Islamic word meaning my sister

SEEKING HELP:

COOKIES highlights the many issues and problems young people may encounter when online. The following organisations can offer advice and support:

Kidscape www.kidscape.org.uk
Information on all forms of bullying both on and offline.

NSPCC www.nspcc.org.uk/preventing-abuse/keeping-children-safe/
The leading children's charity fighting to prevent child abuse in the UK and Channel Islands.

UK Safer Internet Centre www.saferinternet.org.uk
E-safety tips, advice and resources to stay safe online including a helpline for professionals.

IWF Internet Watch Foundation www.iwf.org.uk
An anonymous and safe place to report online child sexual abuse imagery and videos.

VISIT THE SAMUEL FRENCH BOOKSHOP AT THE ROYAL COURT THEATRE

Browse plays and theatre books, get expert advice and enjoy a coffee

Samuel French Bookshop
Royal Court Theatre
Sloane Square
London
SW1W 8AS
020 7565 5024

Shop from thousands of titles on our website

 samuelfrench.co.uk

 samuelfrenchltd

 samuel french uk

Lightning Source UK Ltd.
Milton Keynes UK
UKHW021812051218
333518UK00007B/884/P